MINI-GUIDES

BATTLE
OF NORMANDY......

The German Defeat

August 1st - 29, 1944

Alexandre THERS

Lay-out by the author - Computer drawings by Antoine POGGIOLI
Translated from the French by Jonathan NORTH

PARIS

TOWARDS VICTORY

At dawn on August 1, 1944, the future seemed bright for the Americans. General George S. Patton, tasked with liberating Brittany, was rapidly pushing south from Avranches and his vanguard had even reached the region of Armorica. He was still unaware, however, that the collapse of the German front had created a unique opportunity for him to encircle the enemy still defending Normandy.

*S*leeve badge worn by troops of the British 2nd Army. *(Militaria Magazine)*

···

*R*ight: British generals Montgomery and Dempsey sit between their American counterparts, Bradley (commander, from August 1st, of 12th Army Group) and Hodges (new commander of 1st Army). On August 1st the Allies held a line from Ouisetreham in the north to Avranches in the south. There was a bulge around Caen. This ran from Caumont, forming an enclave to the north-east of Tessy and continued through Percy, Villedieu and Brécey. *(DR)*

But the elimination of the German threat could only occur if their strength was reduced to the utmost. General Dwight D. Eisenhower, Supreme Commander of Allied Expeditionary Forces, requested that the British go back on the offensive in order to keep the Germans focused on the Caen sector thereby presenting Patton and his 3d Army with the best possible opportunities. Field Marshal Bernard L. Montgomery therefore ordered General Dempsey, commanding the British 2nd Army, to attack a relatively undefended sector of the front, between Noyers and the area held by the Americans around Caumont. This area was some distance from the six Panzer divisions

based around Noyers-Bocage, but it wasn't particularly suitable for an offensive. The terrain was rough, broken by a series of ridges, such as Mont Pinçon. This was an ideal observation post for artillery and, like Vire, was an important communications hub. It became one of the chief objec-

*O*pposite: the audacious and aggressive General Patton would reveal his talent for strategic thinking during the exploitation of the Avranches breakthrough. *(National Archives)*

4

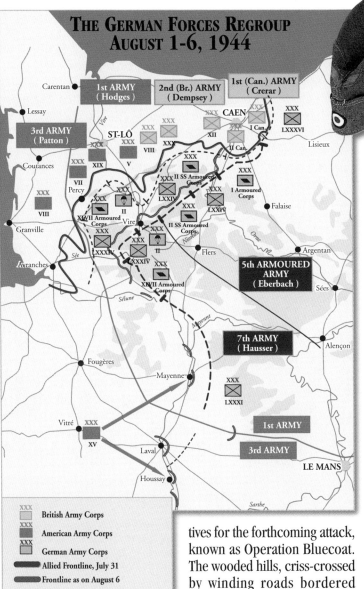

THE GERMAN FORCES REGROUP AUGUST 1-6, 1944

Carentan
Lessay
Coutances
Granville
Avranches
Fougères
Vitré
Houssay

1st ARMY (Hodges)
2nd (Br.) ARMY (Dempsey)
1st (Can.) ARMY (Crerar)
CAEN
Lisieux
3rd ARMY (Patton)
ST-LÔ
Falaise
Argentan
5th ARMOURED ARMY (Eberbach)
Sées
7th ARMY (Hausser)
Alençon
Mayenne
1st ARMY
3rd ARMY
LE MANS
Laval

VII Percy
VIII
XIX
V
VIII
XII
I Can.
II Can.
LXXXVI
II SS Armoured Corps
I Armoured Corps
LXXIV
LXIV
II SS Armoured Corps
XLVII Armoured Corps
LXXXIV
XXXIV
XLVII Armoured Corps
LXXXI
XV

British Army Corps
American Army Corps
German Army Corps
Allied Frontline, July 31
Frontline as on August 6
German Lines, August 1
German Lines, August 6

A German 1934–35 Model fatigue cap. Despite the introduction of a new style of cap in 1943, this older type was common throughout the Normandy campaign. (Militaria Magazine)

General Heinrich Eberbach (on the right) was inspector general of German armored forces before taking over the command of Panzergruppe West on July 3rd 1944. This unit was renamed the 5th Panzer Army on August 5th. (Bundesarchiv)

tives for the forthcoming attack, known as Operation Bluecoat. The wooded hills, criss-crossed by winding roads bordered by thick hedges, were not ideal terrain for tanks.

Below: a German anti-personnel mine, a schrapnellmine 35. (Private Collection)

The German Perspective

Although the situation was catastrophic in the sector around Avranches, German troops held relatively secure positions in other sectors of the front. They opposed the Americans of Major General J. Lawton Collins' VII Corps before Mortain, Major General Charles H. Corlett's XIX Corps before Vire and Major General Leonard T. Gerow's V Corps before Tinchebray. In the British sector, only Generalleutnant Wilhelm Bittrich's 2nd SS Panzer Corps was being subjected to any

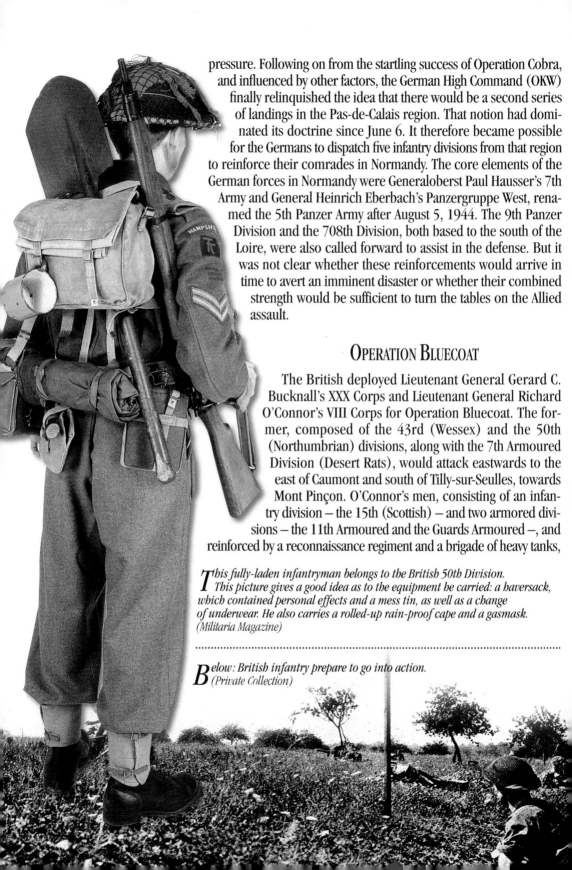

pressure. Following on from the startling success of Operation Cobra, and influenced by other factors, the German High Command (OKW) finally relinquished the idea that there would be a second series of landings in the Pas-de-Calais region. That notion had dominated its doctrine since June 6. It therefore became possible for the Germans to dispatch five infantry divisions from that region to reinforce their comrades in Normandy. The core elements of the German forces in Normandy were Generaloberst Paul Hausser's 7th Army and General Heinrich Eberbach's Panzergruppe West, renamed the 5th Panzer Army after August 5, 1944. The 9th Panzer Division and the 708th Division, both based to the south of the Loire, were also called forward to assist in the defense. But it was not clear whether these reinforcements would arrive in time to avert an imminent disaster or whether their combined strength would be sufficient to turn the tables on the Allied assault.

OPERATION BLUECOAT

The British deployed Lieutenant General Gerard C. Bucknall's XXX Corps and Lieutenant General Richard O'Connor's VIII Corps for Operation Bluecoat. The former, composed of the 43rd (Wessex) and the 50th (Northumbrian) divisions, along with the 7th Armoured Division (Desert Rats), would attack eastwards to the east of Caumont and south of Tilly-sur-Seulles, towards Mont Pinçon. O'Connor's men, consisting of an infantry division – the 15th (Scottish) – and two armored divisions – the 11th Armoured and the Guards Armoured –, and reinforced by a reconnaissance regiment and a brigade of heavy tanks,

This fully-laden infantryman belongs to the British 50th Division. This picture gives a good idea as to the equipment he carried: a haversack, which contained personal effects and a mess tin, as well as a change of underwear. He also carries a rolled-up rain-proof cape and a gasmask. (Militaria Magazine)

Below: British infantry prepare to go into action. (Private Collection)

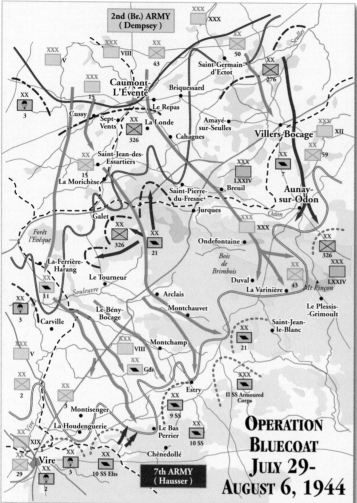

2nd (Br.) ARMY
(Dempsey)

OPERATION
BLUECOAT
JULY 29-
AUGUST 6, 1944

7th ARMY
(Hausser)

*S*leeve badge as worn by troops of the British XXX Corps. (Militaria Magazine)

The German divisions sent as reinforcements from the Pas-de-Calais region were the 84th, 85th, 89th, 331st and 363rd divisions. They were detached from von Salmuth's 15th Army.

A British regulation boot as issued to all British troops with the exception of tank crews and drivers of vehicles. (Militaria Magazine)

....

A British Bren machine-gun, a standard automatic firearm for Commonwealth forces.
(Private Collection)

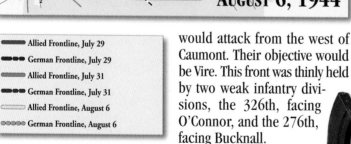

▬▬▬	Allied Frontline, July 29
▬●●●	German Frontline, July 29
▬▬▬	Allied Frontline, July 31
▬●●●	German Frontline, July 31
▭▭▭	Allied Frontline, August 6
○○○○○	German Frontline, August 6

would attack from the west of Caumont. Their objective would be Vire. This front was thinly held by two weak infantry divisions, the 326th, facing O'Connor, and the 276th, facing Bucknall. But the Germans were solidly dug in along wooded heights and had made liberal use of mines. This meant that the British would have to attack along a narrow front clearing a way forward for those following on behind.

On July 30, at 06.00, the 50th Division launched an attack in the Saint-Germain d'Ectot sector. This was followed by another attack, carried out by the 43rd Division, at 08.00. Even though the

British brushed aside weak counter-attacks from the 276th Division progress was not good. The Wessex division managed to seize Briquessard to the west but XXX Corps' furthest point of advance was to be Cahagnes, reached at midnight. On the other hand VIII Corps went further, taking the Lutain woods at 08.30 as well as the village of Sept-Vents. The advance picked up speed and by 15.00 the Guards' tank brigade had achieved all its objectives, seizing the crossroads at Hervieux as well as Hill 226. Meanwhile Hill 309, a key position, was being pulverized by a heavy bombardment. Allied tanks attempted to mount an assault but supporting infantry had not caught up and the tank commander soon realized that, because of XXX Corps' poor progress, his left flank was now exposed. Nevertheless he resolved to push on regardless and seize this crucial feature. The 3rd Battalion Coldstream Guards (Churchill tanks) reached the summit towards 16.00. Resistance had been somewhat sporadic. Over in the sector around Morichesse, however, the Germans now committed Jagdpanthers from schwere Panzer-Jäger-Abteilung 654 which tore into the Allied tanks. The supporting infantry (Glasgow Highlanders) became caught up with the 15th (Scottish) Division and had to march to the front. When they finally got into position they were pinned down by machine-gun fire. The Coldstreams intervened but were ambushed. A few Messerschmitt Bf 109s even strafed the British tanks.

Further to the southwest, the 4th Battalion Scots Guards found themselves in an identical position as they held on to Hill 226, near the Loges, which dominated the Caumont to Saint-Martin-des-Besaces road. At 18.00 three Jagdpanthers burst out of cover near the hill and destroyed 14 Churchills. Two of the German tank-destroyers were knocked out. Hill 226, as well as Hill 309, remained in British hands. The 11th Armoured Division, covering the flank of the 15th (Scottish) Division, had also made con-

A German Army artillery officer. He's using a portable range-finder which would allow him to measure distances and adjust the fire of artillery pieces accordingly. His tunic is made out of the same fabric used for tents and isn't regulation issue.
(Militaria Magazine)

The Jagdpanther was a superb tank-destroyer. Equipped with the legendary Pak 43/3 L/71 88mm anti-tank gun it was one of the most successful types of German armor used in World War II. Just one unit was equipped with these vehicles during the Normandy campaign: the schwere Panzer-Jäger-Abteilung 654. (DR)

siderable progress towards Saint-Martin-des-Besaces and the adjoining ridge. Its 29th Armoured Brigade was caught up in heavy fighting in the woods around Cussy but Saint-Jean-des-Essartiers was seized and, as night fell, the British had reached Dampierre. Contact was made with the American V Corps and, throughout the night, the British pushed on. On July 31, however, a new adversary appeared. The 21st Panzer Division had been much reduced by two months of fighting but had been reinforced by the schwere Panzer-Abteilung 503 with its 13 fearsome Tiger IIs. After an artillery barrage, German troops surged forward to attack the Seaforth Highlanders and Glasgow Highlanders. Two attacks were beaten off but the situation was grave as the British could not hit the Panzers. They could only be stopped by artillery and aircraft; these destroyed some 20 German tanks. Meanwhile, 11th Armoured continued to advance on Saint-Martin-des-

British general O'Connor. He had taken part in the western desert campaigns, being captured by the Germans on April 6, 1941. The Italian armistice, signed in 1943, allowed him to return to Britain. Given command of VIII Corps and sent to Normandy, he didn't show all the abilities he had revealed in Africa. (DR)

The British had excellent artillery. This howitzer is a 4.5, Mk2, 114mm caliber. (Model constructed by Bernard Sailly/SteelMasters)

Besaces. A defensive line was breached and passed and the village was captured towards noon.

The Soleuvre is Crossed

The situation changed considerably when VIII Corps' reconnaissance regiment, having swept unopposed through the Evêque forest, located a gap in the lines between General Meindl's 2nd Fallschirmjäger Corps and General von Choltitz's 84th Corps and was able to reach the Saint-Lô to Bény-Bocage road. The British, taking up a position in the vicinity, discovered an unguarded bridge over the Soleuvre. Using radios, they called up support and a few tanks of the 2nd Northamptonshire Yeomanry were dispatched to guard the bridge. The bridge would be of tremendous significance for subsequent operations as it would enable the 11th Armoured Division to create a bridgehead on the southern bank of the river and strike out in the direction of Vire. As the bridge was being secured, contact was also made with the Americans of V Corps, covering the British right flank, to the south of the Evêque forest.

General O'Connor now ordered the Guards Armoured Division to advance in order to cover 11th Armoured's left flank. The Guards would launch an attack from Saint-Martin-des-Besaces and head south in the direction of Tourneur. Around Hill 309 the 21st Panzer Division, after several assaults in vain, was now pushed back once and for all. Despite enjoying the advantage of the terrain, and the support of the Jagdpanthers and the Tigers, the Germans were on the run and the British, whose artillery had played a crucial role, had the initiative. In XXX Corps' sector engineers had worked hard to free a passage for the British units. That afternoon after a series of clashes, the 43rd Division captured Cahagnes, and later that night, Saint-Pierre-du-Fresne. The 50th Division, by contrast, was stalled.

The German Reaction

The Germans were well aware of their predicament and so decided to commit two armored divisions to the fray. These were the 9th SS Panzer Division (Hohenstaufen) and the 10th SS Panzer Division (Frundsberg) which had been positioned around Caen. The first was intended to

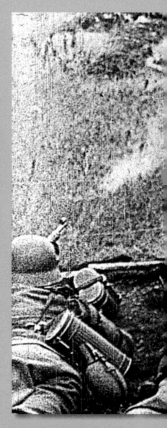

Top left: a Fallschirmjäger badge. The German paratroopers fought as elite infantry throughout the campaign and were not used in their airborne role. (Militaria Magazine)

Top right: Vire in ruins. On August 2, Corlett, commanding the US XIX Corps, began his offensive towards the town. His colleague, Gerow, commander of V Corps, pushed northwards towards the same objective. The Americans met stiff resistance but the town finally fell at dawn on August 7th when the 29th Infantry Division (XIX Corps) and elements of the 2nd Armored broke through. (National Archives)

Opposite: German Puma combat knives. (Private Collection)

10

German forces were organized as follows on the evening of August 6:

5th Panzer Army
86th Corps
- 346th, 272nd, 711th divisions.
1st SS Panzer Corps
- 89th, 271st divisions, 12th SS PzDiv.
74th Corps
- 277th, 276th, 326th divisions.
2nd SS Panzer Corps
- 21st PzDiv., 9th and 10th SS PzDiv.

7th Army
2nd Fallschirmjäger Corps
- 3rd Fallschirmjäger Division, 363rd Division. Elements of 10th SS Panzer Division.
84th Corps
- Kampfgruppen 353rd Division, 243rd, 275th, 84th divisions.
47th Panzer Corps
- 116th, 2nd PzDiv., 1st SS PzDiv., Kampfgruppe 17th PzGren. Div.
81st Corps
- 9th PzDiv., 708th Division, elements of the 5th Fallschirm-jäger Division and the 13th Flak Division.

secure the front around Hill 205 (to the west of Bény-Bocage) and safeguard Tourneur whilst the latter was to attack the British around Aunay-sur-Odon. The Guards had seized Hill 238 at dawn on August 1, but the advance southwards from Saint-Martin-des-Besaces proved difficult as units of the 21st Panzer Division fought back. But, by the end of the day, Tourneur had been reached. The 11th Armoured, having crossed the Souleuvre the day before, now took up a position close to Hill 205. One of its squadrons, pushing through Bény-Bocage, even managed to cut the Caen to Vire road and was just 10 miles from Vire and its garrison of German paratroopers. But progress was not all so straightforward and the British were surprised by the German reaction. Colliding with the vanguard of the Hohenstaufen, O'Connor's men soon found themselves on the defensive against the bulk of the SS division, supported by elements of the Frundsberg. The Germans attacked between Chênedollé and Montchauvet and soon the British were caught up in a series of running battles against small groups of seasoned SS troops. British progress shuddered to a halt. German resistance brought the Bluecoat breakthrough to a close. The SS, reinforced, and linking up with the 3rd Falls-chirmjäger Division, established themselves between Montchauvet and Vire, forming a new defensive line which seemed impregnable

Left: a German machine-gunner fires bursts to support his infantry comrades. (DR)

General Horrocks, despite not having recovered fully from wounds, took over the command of British XXX Corps from Bucknall. (IWM)

to the troops of VIII Corps.

In XXX Corps' sector, the 7th Armoured Division could only maintain a relatively slow pace as it pushed towards Villers-Bocage and Aunay-sur-Odon. Objectives to the north of Mont Pinçon, and all around the height, were not taken. As a result of this failure Bucknall, Major General Robert Erskine, the commander of the 7th Armoured, and two other general officers were dismissed. Lieutenant General Brian Horrocks

Mortain was the principal town of the Manche region. It is seen here before Allied bombers wrought their destruction. (DR)

took over XXX Corps. That same day the Frundsberg division entered combat in strength, destroying 20 tanks.

On August 3 the Germans made a tactical withdrawal, pulling back the 5th Panzer Army in order to allow those units facing the Americans (see the next section) to reorganize. This meant that the British of XXX Corps could enter Villers-Bocage and Aunay-sur-Odon. But resistance continued in VIII Corps' sector. On August 6, the Frundsberg division went on the offensive around Burcy, pushing into a battalion of the 3rd Infantry Division. A single Tiger II, positioned on the Chênedollé heights, caught sight of a column of Shermans descending the heights opposite. It knocked out one tank after another and soon 14 burning wrecks littered the fields. The Germans had established themselves along a line which ran from around Vire, which fell into American hands on the August 7, to Chênedollé and Estry. They would maintain themselves here until August 13. But Operation Bluecoat was over and it just remained for the British to seize Mont Pinçon. At noon on August 6, the infantry and tanks, sweltering in the heat, advanced towards the summit. The Wiltshire Regiment, an exhausted unit held in reserve, was also brought up in support. Aided by a ground mist, the British advanced but the effort was such that the troops literally collapsed of exhaustion and fell right into the abandoned German trenches.

This corporal, a member of the German Army's Panzer arm, wears protective pants and a regulation gray tunic. He wears a particular kind of field cap introduced for tank crews in September 1943. (Militaria Magazine)

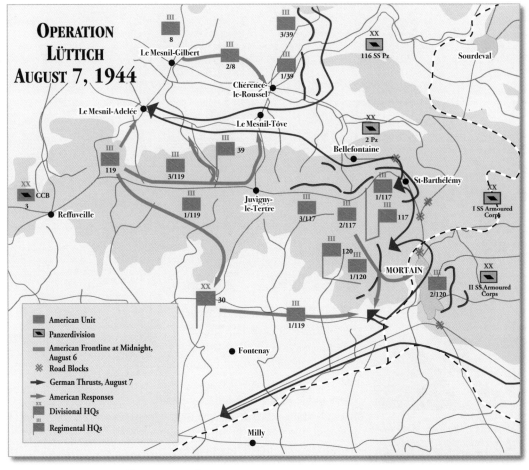

OPERATION LÜTTICH
AUGUST 7, 1944

Le Mesnil-Gilbert
Chérencé-le-Roussel
Le Mesnil-Adelée
Le Mesnil-Tôve
Sourdeval
Bellefontaine
St-Barthélemy
Le Mesnil-Adelée
Reffuveille
Juvigny-le-Tertre
MORTAIN
Fontenay
Milly

116 SS Pz
2 Pz
I SS Armoured Corps
II SS Armoured Corps

Legend
- American Unit
- Panzerdivision
- American Frontline at Midnight, August 6
- Road Blocks
- German Thrusts, August 7
- American Responses
- Divisional HQs
- Regimental HQs

OPERATION LÜTTICH

In the American sector of the front the Allied advance had been irresistible and the way forward was open. Since August 2, Eisenhower had decided to concentrate the bulk of the Allied force on the task of destroying the German forces. The following day, General Omar Bradley informed Patton to only direct a small force against Brittany and to direct the majority of his men against the Germans in the east. With Brittany relegated in importance, Patton's mission was now to advance as far as the Mayenne, push through the town of the same name, and on to Laval. He was then to sweep to the south of the US 1st Army as far as the Loire. Patton therefore dispatched three out of his four Army Corps eastwards (Major General Gilbert R. Cook's XII Corps, Major General Wade H. Haislip's XV Corps, and Major General Walton H. Walker's XX Corps) whilst the remaining Army Corps (Major General Troy H. Middleton's VIII Corps) was loaned to the US 1st Army and given the task of liberating Brittany. Patton's troops now formed the southern arm of the pincer, the British and Canadians

*G*eneral Haislip, one of Patton's subordinates, commanded the US XV Corps. He got across the Mayenne without difficulty, and pushed for Mans, which he took on August 8, whilst his colleague, Walker, headed for Nancy and the Loire. (National Archives)

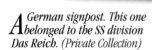

A German signpost. This one belonged to the SS division Das Reich. (Private Collection)

G eneral Hodges was described by Bradley in the following terms: "Whilst Patton rarely got involved with the details, Hodges studied problems with real attention to detail and was more suited to complex operations ... Hodges was the anonymous eminence grise who crushed the German 7th Army whilst Patton circled around it". (DR)

A cap badge from the 116th Panzer Division. It shows a greyhound running. (Militaria Magazine)

forming the northern arm. Caught in the middle was Hausser's 7th Army.

Feldmarschall Günther von Kluge could see the danger and the opportunities which were now presenting themselves to the Allies. If Bradley's men broke through to the south from Argentan and a similar breakthrough was achieved to the north, then the 7th Army would be trapped. In order to avoid this disaster there was just one

A sleeve badge worn by men of the US 30th Infantry Division. The division was commanded by Major General Hobbs. (Militaria Magazine)

plausible alternative: the Germans would have to pull back from Normandy and take up a position along the River Seine. This would inevitably mean a withdrawal to the German border sooner or later. Hitler, after briefly toying with the idea, rejected it. Consequently OKW ordered von Kluge to launch a counter-attack as soon as possible. The Germans were to attack from Mortain, ten miles to the south of Vire, with the intention of reaching Avranches on the coast, thereby cutting the US 3rd Army in two and depriving it of its supplies. The Germans would then swing northwards and tackle the US 1st Army. The plan, drawn up by Hitler himself, was certainly audacious. But where would the Germans be able to find the necessary troops to carry out such a scheme successfully? The only available troops were General Hans von Funck's 47th Panzer Corps stationed close by Mortain. Its 2nd Panzer Division, along with the 2-SS Panzer (Das Reich) would form the spearhead for the attack, reinforced by the 116th Panzer Division. The 9th Panzer Division, expected in the sec-

A German Panzer V Panther type G, the best German tank of the period. (Model and photo by Frédéric Astier/SteelMasters)

tor at any moment, was also to participate. The Germans also hoped to make use of 1-SS Panzer Division (Leibstandarte SS-Adolf Hitler) and the 12-SS Panzer Division (Hitlerjugend) as these were based around Caen and that sector of the front was much quieter now.

At 01.00 on August 3, Hitler finally consented to the retreat of the 5th Panzer Army so that it could reform. As we have seen, the redeployment of this unit allowed the British to enter Villers-Bocage and Aunay. As far as von Kluge was concerned, the coming offensive was totally unrealistic in its aims as it would inevitably weaken the other sectors of the front, rendering them vulnerable to further Allied attacks. But he was now the hostage of a Führer directive, a leader more and more suspicious of his generals since the July 20th bomb plot. Von Kluge could only inform his skeptical subordinates that it was a Führer order. Von Kluge now focused on retaking, and this time holding, Avranches. There were complications and preparations were marred because 9th Panzer Division had still not arrived. But von Kluge planned the operation, codenamed Lüttich, so that the Germans would carry out a three-pronged assault between the Sée and the Sélune. In the north, on the German right flank, the 116th Panzer Division would attack along the northern bank of the Sée. In the center, the 2nd Panzer Division, reinforced by two tank battalions, would sweep along the southern bank. In the south, 2-SS Panzer Division, reinforced by 17-SS Panzergrenadier Division (Götz von Berlichingen), would form the right flank of the attack and engage Allied units around Mortain. Finally the Leibstandarte was to be kept in reserve in order to exploit any breakthrough. Of course these troops were just a small part of those requested. Just a few hours before the offensive was scheduled to begin, Hitler finally consented to allow further troops, such as the 11th Panzer Division based in the south of France, to participate. Getting the troops forward to their points of departure proved problematic and the confusion was such that the commander of the 47th Corps asked for the postponement of the operation. Von Kluge's

A rocket fired from an Allied fighter-bomber. Such missiles could pierce armor but they were inaccurate. (DR)

A German infantryman's assault equipment. It consisted of a mess tin and a tent sheet. (Militaria Magazine)

15

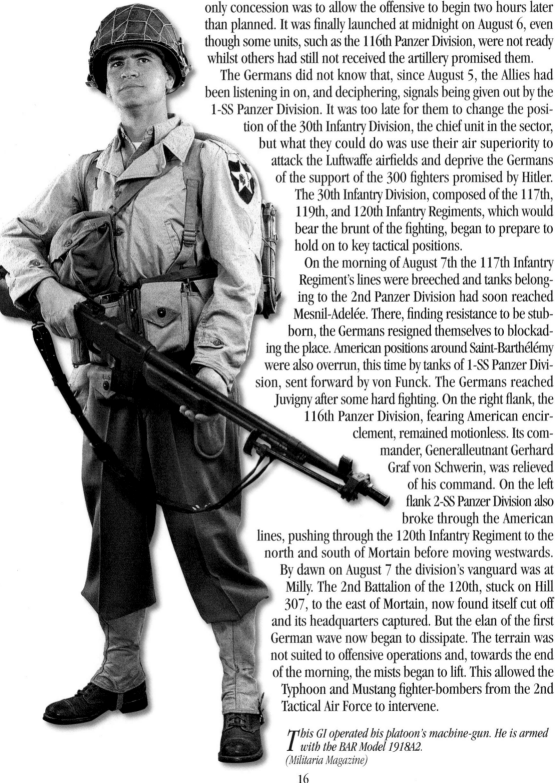

only concession was to allow the offensive to begin two hours later than planned. It was finally launched at midnight on August 6, even though some units, such as the 116th Panzer Division, were not ready whilst others had still not received the artillery promised them.

The Germans did not know that, since August 5, the Allies had been listening in on, and deciphering, signals being given out by the 1-SS Panzer Division. It was too late for them to change the position of the 30th Infantry Division, the chief unit in the sector, but what they could do was use their air superiority to attack the Luftwaffe airfields and deprive the Germans of the support of the 300 fighters promised by Hitler.

The 30th Infantry Division, composed of the 117th, 119th, and 120th Infantry Regiments, which would bear the brunt of the fighting, began to prepare to hold on to key tactical positions.

On the morning of August 7th the 117th Infantry Regiment's lines were breeched and tanks belonging to the 2nd Panzer Division had soon reached Mesnil-Adelée. There, finding resistance to be stubborn, the Germans resigned themselves to blockading the place. American positions around Saint-Barthélémy were also overrun, this time by tanks of 1-SS Panzer Division, sent forward by von Funck. The Germans reached Juvigny after some hard fighting. On the right flank, the 116th Panzer Division, fearing American encirclement, remained motionless. Its commander, Generalleutnant Gerhard Graf von Schwerin, was relieved of his command. On the left flank 2-SS Panzer Division also broke through the American lines, pushing through the 120th Infantry Regiment to the north and south of Mortain before moving westwards. By dawn on August 7 the division's vanguard was at Milly. The 2nd Battalion of the 120th, stuck on Hill 307, to the east of Mortain, now found itself cut off and its headquarters captured. But the elan of the first German wave now began to dissipate. The terrain was not suited to offensive operations and, towards the end of the morning, the mists began to lift. This allowed the Typhoon and Mustang fighter-bombers from the 2nd Tactical Air Force to intervene.

This GI operated his platoon's machine-gun. He is armed with the BAR Model 1918A2.
(Militaria Magazine)

Men besieged on Hill 307 were sent morphine, bottles of plasma, and bandages. These were fired at them by the American artillery, the medicines being placed in hollow shells originally designed to send pamphlets into the German lines. (Militaria Mag.)

The British Air Marshal, Leigh-Mallory, directed aircraft attached to the Allied expeditionary force as well as the US 9th Air Force. This force was perhaps the greatest aerial armada ever assembled. It proved decisive for Allied success in Normandy. (Militaria Magazine)

Congestion on the narrow roads was such that the tanks found it almost impossible to break for cover. They didn't fear the Typhoon's guns but the rockets these planes carried on their wings were deadly, if inaccurate. Finally, American artillery came into play and German losses began to mount. Das Reich found itself trapped a mile from Saint-Hilaire du Harcouet. The air raids were beginning to intensify and so, around noon, von Funck decided to call off the offensive, but Hitler, despite knowing that the Allies were now also on the offensive, insisted in redirecting reinforcements to aid the German offensive. Transferring the Hohenstaufen, Frundsberg and Hitlerjugend would fatally weaken other sectors of the front but these were now ordered forward in an attempt to succeed where the 2nd Panzer Division had failed. Even though the German commanders on the ground were only too aware that their lines could collapse at any moment, the offensive was renewed on August 8. To the east of Avranches the 700 remaining men of the 2nd Battalion of the 120th, holding on to Hill 307, were causing the Das Reich considerable trouble. The Americans were using their artillery to fire on the German communications, significantly impeding their process. The following day Douglas C-47 Skytrain (Dakota) transports managed to re-supply their besieged comrades from the air. But only on August 12 did men from the 35th Infantry Division break through to relieve the 300

On August 11 the Allies finalized their operational plan. A division belonging to the US XV Corps would leave Mans and push north towards Alençon and Argentan. The Canadian 1st Army would first take Falaise and then head for Argentan. The British 2nd Army and the US 1st Army would then squeeze the pocket thereby created. Von Kluge, informed by his intelligence services of these plans, hoped to counter-attack towards Alençon. There could be no operation against Argentan.

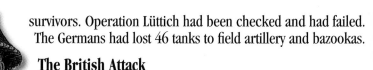

survivors. Operation Lüttich had been checked and had failed. The Germans had lost 46 tanks to field artillery and bazookas.

The British Attack

All von Kluge's worst fears were coming true. The Americans had begun a vast turning movement and were now pushing northwards from Alençon, heading towards the British and Canadians and threatening to surround the 7th Army around Falaise. If this Army was destroyed, the Germans would have nothing left with which to oppose the Allies. Now Montgomery also began to pressure the enemy. While troops of the 12th Army Group were dispatched towards Paris, the 1st (Canadian) Army was tasked with taking Falaise as part of Operation Totalize.

OPERATION TOTALIZE

Diverting armored divisions away from the sector south of Caen so that they could participate in the attack around Mortain had weakened the German lines in that area. The tanks were replaced by infantry divisions. Even so the anti-tank artillery which had inflicted such heavy losses on the British armor during Operation Goodwood was still in position. Despite this apparent handicap, Montgomery was convinced that an attack on Falaise stood a good chance of success. Lieutenant General Harry D.G. Crerar, commander of the 1st (Canadian) Army, was entrusted with the mission. On the ground the details were left to Lieutenant General Guy G. Simonds, commanding II (Canadian) Corps. Simonds had carefully noted how and why previous British attacks had failed and how he could deploy his forces to overcome the obstacles set before him. He realized that he had to allow the infantry the chance to keep up with the tanks and that the latter should arrive in good physical condition. He also knew that infantry and tanks should be brought into contact with the German lines quickly so as to prevent the Germans from reacting and that armored units should be given maximum fire support and not have to wait for artillery in order to exploit a breakthrough.

This Canadian officer wears a combat uniform. He is a lieutenant in the Regina Rifle Regiment (3rd Canadian Division) and wears the 1937 combat uniform. He has brown leather boots. (Militaria Magazine)

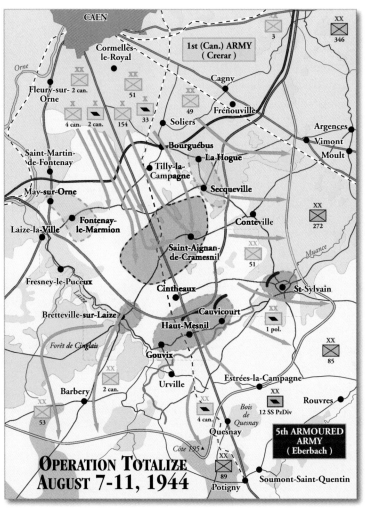

CAEN

1st (Can.) ARMY (Crerar)

XX 3

XX 346

Cormelles-le-Royal

Orne

Fleury-sur-Orne 2 can.

XX 51

Cagny

49

Soliers

Frénouville

4 can. 2 can. 154 33

Argences

Vimont

Moult

Bourguébus

La Hogue

Saint-Martin-de-Fontenay

Tilly-la-Campagne

Secqueville

May-sur-Orne

Fontenay-le-Marmion

Laize-la-Ville

Conteville

XX 272

Fresney-le-Puceux

Saint-Aignan-de-Cramesnil

XX 51

Muance

Cintheaux

St-Sylvain

Bretteville-sur-Laize

Cauvicourt

Haut-Mesnil

1 pol.

Forêt de Cinglais

Gouvix

XX 85

Barbery

XX 2 can.

Urville

Estrées-la-Campagne

XX 4 can.

Bois de Quesnay

Rouvres

XX 12 SS PzDiv

XX 53

Quesnay

5th ARMOURED ARMY (Eberbach)

Côte 195

XX 89

Potigny

Soumont-Saint-Quentin

ØPERATION TOTALIZE
AUGUST 7-11, 1944

Simonds came to the conclusion that a night attack was
the best way to surmount these problems. A compact
mass of tanks, followed by motorized infantry, should
be able to break through the German lines.

*B*ritish artillery binoculars,
Mark II 7 x 7. (Militaria Magazine)

▬▬▬	Allied Frontline, August 7
▬▬▬	Allied Frontline, August 8
▬▬▬	Allied Frontline, August 11
▬▬▬	German Reserves
▨	Objectives for Bombers, night of August 7
▨	Objectives for Bombers, August 8
▨	German Defensive Zone

*B*ottom left : insignia worn
on the sleeves of troops
belonging to the Canadian
2nd Armoured Brigade.
(Militaria Magazine)

*B*ottom left : a Kangaroo troop
transporter. This vehicle was
in effect either a modified Priest
self-propelled gun or a modified
Canadian Ram tank. (IWM)

*A*British
entrenching
tool. It could
be fitted with a Mark II
bayonet and used
to detect mines.
(Militaria Magazine)

In order to maximize the effect of surprise, an artillery barrage was ruled out. Simonds' plan called for the creation of illuminated tracks so that the tanks would not stray from their objectives in the dark. In order to do this various methods were considered. Searchlights for artificial moonlight, flares, tracer bullets, the use of Flail tanks fitted with direction finders to lead the way, all these were discussed. Allied air forces were also called upon to make their contribution. They would pummel German fortifications along the Caen to Falaise road during the offensive before switching to blasting a path through German defenses in the rear. Pilots were called upon to fly as many missions as possible in order to attack as many targets as possible with bombs and rockets.

Getting the troops forward at the same time as the tanks was made possible by the ingeneous conversion of over a 100 Priest self-propelled guns into armored personnel carriers. On August 6, while battle raged around Mortain, the British and Canadians launched a series of probing attacks around Troarn, creating a bridgehead at Grimbosq on the Orne, to the south of Caen, which distracted Dietrich's 1-SS Panzer Corps and the Hitlerjugend. Meanwhile, the offensive launched by the British 2nd Army to the south of Caumont sucked in the rest of the German armor – namely 2-SS Panzer Corps and the 21st Panzer Division. Now was the time to act. The operation would be launched on August 7. That evening, preceded by engineer special tanks, four columns rolled forwards along a 70-yard front. The Canadian 4th Brigade and 2nd Armoured Brigade advanced to the left of Route Nationale 158, heading for Cramesnil and Saint-Aignan. The British 51st Infantry Division and 33rd Armoured Brigade attacked along the right of the road. At 22.55 the bombing began with heavy bombers raiding May, Fontenay, La Hogue, Secqueville, Garcelles and Saint-Aignan. But

Top left: a beret belonging to a British tank crewman. This black, woolen beret was first issued in 1924. This beret carries the insignia of an officer of the Royal Tank Regiment. (Militaria Magazine)

....

Above: a Boeing B-17 Flying Fortress. Along with the B-24, the B-17 provided the backbone of the 9th Air Force's might and they intervened powerfully during Operation Totalize. (DR)

....

Opposite: a Sherman M4A4 tank belonging to the Canadian 2nd Armoured Brigade. In total, nearly 1,000 tanks of all kinds were employed during Operation Totalize. (Model and photo by Ludovic Fortin/SteelMasters)

smoke reduced visibility to such an extent that orders were issued to cancel the air raids. A German smokescreen added to the problem and there were soon friendly fire incidents. Nevertheless, progress was good and a few German units broke and fled. At Cintheaux the newly-arrived 89th Division collapsed and the 272nd Division was destroyed.

Standartenführer Kurt Meyer of the Hitlerjugend division reacted with his usual energy. As soon as the bombing ended he went up the Caen to Falaise road, rallying stragglers and assigning troops to defensive positions. He supported the infantry with artillery and a few guns, formed some Kampfgruppen and launched counter-attacks to the north of Cintheaux. These barely managed to save the tanks which had been stuck in the village before the bombers dropped their load. The German tank ace Wittmann was killed during this action.

Meanwhile the Canadians pushed on and their objectives fell one by one: Gaumesnil, Caillouet, Rocquancourt and Hill 122. But the Kampfgruppen, supported by schwere SS-Panzer-Abteilung 101, inflicted heavy casualties on the Canadians. Fontenay was the scene of a particularly fierce battle, as was May-sur-Orne where the Fusiliers Mont Royal suffered heavy losses. Only the intervention of flame-

A case containing German Granatwerfer 34 mortar rounds. (Private Collection)

A British Mills grenade, No 36M. (Private Collection)

throwing tanks led to the eradication of the German defenders. By now it was 05.00 on August 8. The British took Saint-Aignan-de-Cramesnil but faced stiff resistance from the stronghold of Tilly. At dawn the German position was finally breached. Garcelles, Secqueville and the Conteville woods fell to the British. By dawn the British and Canadians had advanced some three miles, making the first phase of the operation a success. But the Canadians had suffered heavily.

The Canadian Offensive Stalls

During August 8, the 51st (Highland) Division, positioned around Bras-Soliers, were relieved by Major General Stanislaw Maczek's 1st Polish Armoured Division. The Poles were to advance with the 4th (Canadian) Armoured Division on Falaise in order to exploit the breakthrough. This second phase was begun when 492 four-engine bombers carried out a massive raid at 12.35. The two armoured divisions launched their attack at 13.55. The Canadians reached the quarry at Hautmesnil by the evening, marking the furthest point of the Allied advance. Further west, Bretteville-sur-Laize was taken but many Canadian tanks were destroyed by 88mm Flak guns. As for the Poles they were introduced to the SS of the Hitlerjugend in fighting to the east of Saint-Aignan. By the evening both armored divisions were a long cry from their objectives. They took up defensive positions, allowing the Germans time to stabilize their front.

The violence increased on August 9 and 10. The Poles were given the task of taking Cauvicourt and Hautmesnil whilst the 4th Armoured was to take Bretteville-le-Rabet and Hill 195. Hill 195 was to be hit

Opposite: a German Feldfunk Sprecher B transmitter-receiver. These models were for use in the field at company level or battalion level. (Van Onsem Collection)

by two columns led by Major General F.F. Worthington and Lieutenant William W. Halpenny. The attack began at 04.00 but due to some ground mist visibility was poor and Worthington's column got lost. By mistake it positioned itself on another height which it took to be Hill 195. Then it was hit by tanks of Kampfgruppe Wünsche (12-SS Panzer Division), and bombarded by mortar fire. Some 43 Canadian tanks were destroyed. Meanwhile, the Germans pulled back in good order. This retreat allowed the 10th Brigade to seize the actual Hill 195, as well as Hill 206, the following night. Simonds, anxious to continue Operation Totalize, ordered that the Laison be crossed and that the Allies push towards Olendon. But the stubborn resistance of German combat teams, especially in the Quesnay woods, meant that offensive operations stalled despite the Canadians superiority in numbers. As night

An American M1 carbine, 7.62mm caliber. This firearm was designed to fill the gap between a rifle and a pistol. Lighter than a rifle it was issued to troops for whom it would prove to be less of an encumbrance. (Vincey Museum Collection)

A German Waffen SS camouflaged helmet cover. (Militaria Magazine)

Preceding page, top: a German Pak 43/41 88mm anti-tank gun destroyed between Tilly-la-Campagne and Saint-Aignan. (IWM)

Opposite : Shermans belonging to the US 5th Armored. Division. (National Archives)

fell on August 10, the battle was over and the Germans remained masters of the battlefield. Totalize had seen local successes but had not brought the breakthrough which had been hoped for. Ten miles had been taken in two days but the enemy had only deployed 45 tanks to resist the onslaught. The Allies had deployed 600.

LECLERC ARRIVES

Meanwhile, Patton had issued orders on August 10th for the US XV Corps (5th Armored and 83rd, 78th and 80th infantry divisions),

A column of Shermans belonging to the 1st Polish Armored Division. (IWM B 8823)

Fighting in support of and along side the Allied forces in Normandy were the following: the 1st Independent Czechoslovak Armored Brigade, fighting as part of the British 51st Division; the Dutch Princess Irene Brigade, which disembarked at Courseulles-sur-Mer on August 6 and which fought at Bréville, Pont-l'Evêque, Benoit, Beuzeville and Pont-Audemer; and the Belgian Piron Brigade which also disembarked at Courseulles, on August 7, and fought along the Orne and the Seine.

August 1, 1944 was an important date in French history. General Leclerc's 2ᵉ Division Blindée landed at Utah Beach following intensive training in Britain. Attached to Patton's XV Corps, it had a strength of 16,200, 244 tanks and 4,000 vehicles (of which 75 were armored cars, 36 were tank-destroyers and 36 self-propelled 105mm howitzers). The division was split into three tactical groupings: the Groupe Tactique Dio, the Groupe Tactique de Langlade and the Groupe Tactique de Guillebon.
The division first went into action on August 8. The following day it was at Château-Gontier. It took Alençon on the 12th before heading for Argentan and participating in the battles of the Falaise pocket (Ecouves forest, Carrouges and Ecouché). The division was then transferred to V Corps, 1st US Army.

....

*M*ain picture: general Leclerc on August 1. He's just about to leave Utah Beach followed by his staff officers. (National Archives)

....

*T*op left: insignia worn by the 2ᵉ Division Blindée. Initially they were manufactured by Cartier of London. They were first issued on June 21st 1944. (Militaria Magazine)

....

*T*op left: sleeve patch worn by men of the US XV Corps. (Militaria Magazine)

....

*T*op right: a French fatigue cap of the kind worn by a captain of the liberating forces. (D. Corbonnois Collection)

25

as well as the French 2e Division Blindée (Armored Division) to attack northwards and seize Alençon. On August 11th the French, with the US 90th Infantry Division following on behind attacked along the Alençon to Carrouges axis whilst 5th Armored moved up with the 79th Infantry Division. Facing them were what remained of diverse

Above: a Tiger tank among the ruins of Falaise. This one belongs to the schwere SS-Panzer-Abteilung 102, a heavy battalion attached to the 2nd SS Panzer Corps. It was sent to positions north of the town on August 9th but lost a number of its tanks during the subsequent retreat.(©ECPAD/France)

Top right : insignia worn on the sleeve of a Luftwaffe driver. Flak guns played an important role in the fighting around Falaise.(PS Collection)

Opposite: A German SPW 251 destroyed by a hit to its rear. German columns had their freedom of movement severely restricted by the closing in of Allied armor. (National Archives)

German divisions, such as the 9th Panzer and the 708th along with odd units from the 352nd and the Panzer Lehr. The Sarthe, to the east of Alençon, was quickly reached and the town itself fell to the 2e Division Blindée which chased out the 116th Panzer Division and elements of the Das Reich on the morning of August 12. Meanwhile, Mamers and Sées welcomed 5th Armored as liberators. Haislip then ordered the fiery commander of the 2e Division Blindée (Général Leclerc) to clear the Ecouves forest, to the south of Argentan. The French division attempted to use a road reserved for the Americans, caused a massive jam and brought 5th Armored to a halt. The Germans used the opportunity to slip away and prepare Argentan's defenses. That same day, Eberbach took charge of the sector. He hoped to organize an armored force against XV Corps's vanguard. The unit Eberbach fashioned was named after him – Panzergruppe Eberbach – and Dietrich took over command of 5th Panzer Army. But the Americans were near and Eberbach had to quickly deploy his troops to halt their progress. The first elements of the 116th Panzer Division on the spot were sent to Argentan to bolster its defense. General Eberbach, however, still hoped to gather enough tanks to strike eastwards and secure the sector around Mortagne before swinging north and crushing the Allies there. But the Panzer units were weighed down by insurmountable difficulties: lack of fuel, clogged roads, and air raids. The German assembly points were constantly being overrun before the Panzers could reach them and the offensive was canceled.

On the morning of August 13, the 2e Division Blindée seized Carrouges and Ecouché. A French patrol even penetrated into Argentan. The outskirts of the town were securely held and it was the point which marked the meeting of Patton's zone of operations and that of the British. Patton, carrying out Bradley's orders, pulled back all to the north of the town. This was unfortunate as the vanguard of XV Corps was now just 20 miles from Falaise and had the opportunity to link with the British. The decision would have grave consequences.

T his man is a member of a Hitlerjugend tank crew. He wears black leather protective overalls. These were originally issued to the German navy and were not standard issue; even so they were popular among men of the 1st SS Panzer Corps in Normandy. Uncomfortable in hot weather, they did at least afford a measure of protection against burning oil.
(Militaria Magazine)

CLOSING THE ARGENTAN-FALAISE POCKET
AUGUST 17-19, 1944

1st (Can.) ARMY

2nd ARMY

2 Can.

Falaise

53

59

Condé-sur-Noireau 43

50

276

277

271

89

326

5th ARMOURED
ARMY

Noireau

3

11

Putanges

Flers 363

7th ARMY

Panzergruppe
Eberbach

1 SS

353

Elms

KG

76

708

84

10 SS

2

KG

275

9

3

1

Râ

La Ferté-Macé

1st ARM

(Until August 1?)

- ●●● Frontlines, Evening of August 16
- ◐◑◐ Positions reached August 17
- ●●●● Positions reached August 18
- ●● ● Positions reached August 19
- → Direction of Polish
  and Canadian Armored Thrust
- ⊗ Contact Points
  of Allied Reconnaissance
- 🏴 HQ of German 7th Army,
  August 19

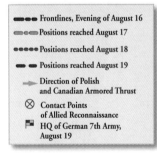

Above: this image shows the tank crew of the Royal Scots Greys (4th Armoured Brigade) resting near Falaise. No British armored unit actually fought in this sector.
(DR)

OPERATION TRACTABLE : THE BATTLE FOR FALAISE

Operation Totalize came to an end on August 9. The 1st (Canadian) Army spent the next couple of days reorganizing so that it could continue with its push towards Falaise. This prime objective was to be taken by the 4th Armoured Division, the 3rd Division and the 4th (Canadian) Armoured Division. The plan was essentially based on Totalize but the tanks would be used in compact masses. The offensive would be supported again by massive air bombings.

On the night before the attack (scheduled for Aug. 14), a Canadian reconnaissance vehicle lost its way and the Allied plan fell into enemy hands. With the few hours remaining the German commanders hastily did what they could. Just before noon the bombing began, hitting the area between Assy and Rouvres. Under the cover of smoke, hundreds of tanks began to surge southwards. Towards 14.00 German lines between Quesnay and Potigny were again pulverized, this time by 800 heavy bombers. The German lines were beginning

O pposite: general Maczek's 1st Polish Armoured Division disembarked on August 1. Attached to the Canadian 1st Army, Maczek's troops played an important part in sealing the Falaise pocket. (IWM)

T he ruins of Argentan. Taking the town was an essential part of sealing the pocket. It fell to the Allies on August 21. (National Archives)

....

B ottom: a British Austin K5 3 ton 4x4 truck belonging to the British 2nd Army. Such vehicles performed a variety of roles and they could also be used to tow artillery. (Model built by B. Sailly/ SteelMasters)

to crumble and 1,000 men, mostly belonging to the 85th Division, were captured. By evening Falaise was just three miles away. The attacks continued on the following day but now German resistance was stiffer, the Hitler-jugend, to the north of Falaise, proving stubborn opponents. That evening Canadians of the 2nd Division were less than half a mile from the town. On August 16 the 4th Armoured Division took Morteaux-Couliboeuf and the Poles reached Neauphe-sur-Dives. Falaise was reached on the morning of the August 17 and by evening was almost entirely in Allied hands. Churchill flame-throwing tanks helped mop up the following day. but the SS fought to the death.

The Germans Surrounded

American progress was not only preventing Eberbach from counter-attacking the US XV Corps but it was also threatening the 7th Army with encirclement. Von Kluge, who was attempting to organize a counter-attack, had to change tack on August 13 and hastily asked to withdraw Panzergruppe Eberbach and 7th Army. But Hitler refused, fearing that Chartres and Dreux, 30 miles to the east of Falaise might be threatened. He ordered Panzergruppe Eberbach to strike southwards, towards Carrouges thereby isolating the American corps. The only concession von Kluge was able to extract was that units positioned to the west of Trun might withdraw so that the armored units could move up and attack. Von Kluge therefore ordered 2-SS Panzer Corps to link up with Panzergruppe Eberbach. But the Canadian offensive of August 14 against Falaise called into question the feasibility of an offensive by 1-SS Panzer Corps against the XV Corps.

The next morning, von Kluge set off to see Eberbach and Hausser, commander of 7th Army, at Nécy. Attacked by Allied fighter-bombers, his vehicle radio was knocked out and he only reached Eberbach's headquarters that evening. Meanwhile, not knowing what had happened to von Kluge, Hausser had temporarily placed himself in command of Army Group B (to which Panzergruppe Eberbach and 7th Army belonged) and Dietrich had made the decision to pull German forces back behind the Dives.

On August 16th, von Kluge sent an urgent message to Generaloberst Alfred Jodl, the Wehrmacht's chief of staff, stressing that it would be impossible to launch any attack. He hoped to convince Jodl that there was no other option but to retreat. Jodl, however, was of the opinion that only a widening of the twenty-mile-wide bottleneck between Argentan and Falaise, by attacking from Argentan towards the Sées, would

*M*echanized infantrymen were an essential part of the German Army's armored divisions. This man wears a camouflage smock different from those used by the Waffen SS. He carries a semi-automatic rifle, Model 1941. This was a rare firearm and was only issued, in theory, at the rate of one per combat section. (Militaria Magazine)

allow for such a move. He decided to refer the matter to Hitler. By 14.39, von Kluge was still waiting and therefore took it upon himself to order a retreat to positions behind the Orne. Hitler's orders arrived two hours later. He accepted a retreat behind the Dives was inevitable but Falaise had to be held and the bottleneck had to be widened by means of an attack from Argentan (still in German hands). So Hitler's orders didn't really contradict von Kluge's and the evacuation of the Falaise pocket could begin. Just as Falaise fell to the Allies, on August 16, the German retreat began.

The German Retreat

On August 13th, Bradley arrived before Argentan. He was convinced he could commence the second phase of the plan drawn up with Montgomery: a push to the Seine.

He ordered Patton to launch part of XV Corps towards the Seine. The 5th Armored and 79th Infantry Divisions moved out on August 15 and on the 16th, had reached Dreux. That same day, Montgomery, not knowing what the Americans had achieved, asked Bradley to send XV Corps to the north of Argentan to link up with the Canadians. The bottleneck no longer lay between Falaise and Argentan, now it had been squeezed to a width of five miles between Chambois and Trun. The pocket measured 25 miles by 12 miles and held more than 100,000 German troops. Bradley therefore decided to use elements of the 1st US Army to attack towards Chambois.

The next day, von Kluge, who was suspected by Hitler of conducting secret negotiations with the Allies, was sacked and replaced by Feldmarschall Walter Model. Hitler also consented that the German retreat over the Orne should continue. One of the Model's first decisions was to reorganize the debris of the 84th, 85th, 89th and 271st divisions into a Kampfgruppe and the other four divisions into another such unit.

Meanwhile, Montgomery went in for the kill and sent in the 1st Polish Armoured Division and the 4th Canadian Armoured Division against the retreating Germans. The enemy, knowing all too well the gravity of the situation, summoned up all they had in order to attempt an evacuation of the pocket. The first phase, on the night of August 16, was carried out in an orderly manner. The same move the following night was much more difficult because of American artillery. It seemed as though the retreat over the Orne might just have worked. But, in the northern sector, the Canadians took Trun and the Poles were less than half a mile from Chambois. The fall of Chambois would cut one of the most important escape routes. To the south the pocket remained open and the retreat continued in good order during the night of August 18. By the following morning, the pocket had been reduced to an area 6 by 7 miles. It held pitiful remnants of the 1st and 12th SS Panzer

The German 89th Division was one of those dispatched from the Pas-de-Calais region. It had an effective strength of 8,000 men. On August 3 it was attached to the 1st SS Panzer Corps. One of its regiments fought in the area around Falaise and Bretteville along with a battalion of tank-destroyers and artillery detachment. A second regiment fought around Thiberville, deploying its Fusiliers and artillery, whilst a third artillery detachment saw action to the south of Lisieux.

On August 20, 1944, just as the German front collapsed, Luftwaffe fighters were present in much greater numbers than they had been at the start of the fighting: 581 Focke-Wulf 190s and Bf 109s. German fighter pilots, who frequently fought outnumbered ten against one, notched up 1,200 victories during the campaign.
(DR)

*F*eldmarschall Model replaced
von Kluge as commander-in-
chief of German forces in the west
and commander of Army Group B.
He showed considerable energy
and a rare talent for improvisation.
He was capable in defense as well
as in offensive action. (DR)

----

*R*ight: German soldbuch
(pay book) issued
to a member of the Waffen SS.
The soldier it was issued to had
to carry it about his person.
(Militaria Magazine)

----

*B*elow: German prisoners
of war captured during
the operations around Falaise.
The delay in closing the pocket
between Argentan and Falaise
meant that some 40,000
Germans evaded captivity
or death. Total German casualties
in Normandy amounted
to 210,000 dead, wounded
and missing. (DR)

Bradley's
unfortunate
decision not
to allow
the XV Corps
to close the circle around
the German 7th and 5th Armies
was based on the assumption
that he could carry out an even
more ambitious encirclement
by reaching the left bank
of the Seine.

divisions, the 2nd and 116th Panzer divisions as well as the Das Reich division, six infantry divisions, a paratroop division and a number of army and corps staffs. The 90th US Infantry Division and Leclerc's men reached Chambois and joined up with the 10th Polish Mounted Rifles. To the North, Canadians of the 4th Armoured Division reached Saint-Lambert. The Poles took Mont Ormel, a key objective and observation post alongside the German avenue of retreat. Meanwhile, the Germans had completed their preparations for breaking out over the Dives. They aimed to hit a point between Trun and Chambois, seize Mont Ormel and keep open a corridor.

At dawn on August 20, the Poles observed German convoys converging from all directions. They were first hit by the Das Reich and soon lost control of two roads. There were numerous clashes that afternoon, and the 2nd Fallschirmjäger Corps and the 47th Panzer Corps managed to break the Allied stranglehold by the evening of the 20th. The 2nd Panzer Division and the Leibstandarte SS-Adolf Hitler were saved, as well as the Frundsberg division. But the 74th and 84th Corps had to fight their way through to the Dives. The former, composed almost solely of the Hitlerjugend, only managed to get its motorized units through. The latter was frustrated and its commander, Generalleutnant Otto Elfeldt, who had replaced von Choltitz, was captured near Saint-Lambert. A few other units managed to break out but the flow of German units out of the pocket began to dry up. The last to leave did so around 16.00 on August 21. The battle of the Falaise pocket was over.

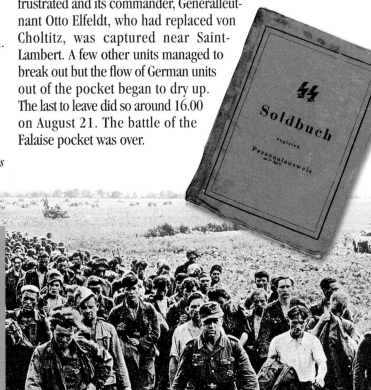

Towards the Seine

The battles around Falaise marked the end of the campaign for Normandy. Those German divisions brought up from the Pas-de-Calais or from other areas had, at best, only managed to delay the Allied advance. The units which escaped from the pocket now began a long retreat to the Seine, in order to save as many men as possible for the defense of Germany. Eisenhower and Montgomery, on the other hand, hoped that the 12th Army Group would pin the Germans against the river whilst the 21st would smash into them.

Meanwhile the Allied commanders directed their air forces to attack depots to the north of the Seine rather than bridges over the river. The weather also played into German hands and they made the most of a period of two days and six nights in which there were no raids. Under Model's careful scrutiny, the Germans formed a pocket on the left bank of the river with Panzergruppe Eberbach resting its left flank on the Eure and Avre and its right flank on the Touques and the Risle. It was there that those troops which had escaped were to be directed whilst Model concentrated the armored units at Evreux. With the exception of a railroad bridge at Rouen, no other crossing point had been left intact north of Paris. Barges and boats of all kinds were gathered in. Meanwhile the roads were terribly congested with men and vehicles but they had little to fear other than Allied pilots.

Meanwhile XV Corps began to advance along the Eure while, on the other side of the river, XIX Corps began to advance from Verneuil, pushing towards Elbeuf and a hoped for a link up with 2nd (Canadian) Corps. The British XXX Corps reached the Seine at Vernon. In fact the river was no real obstacle and it was soon crossed at numerous points by boat and three pontoon bridges were quickly constructed. Just about all the German units which had escaped from Falaise had crossed over the river and, combined with other units located in northern France, amounted to 240,000 men, 30,000 vehicles and 135 tanks. The retreat had been a success. The American attempt to surround the retreating Germans had been launched too late, with insufficient forces and without air support. It had been a failure. But the way open to Paris, and the German frontier, now lay wide open.

The German retreat towards the Seine as seen from above (this is the village of Clinchamps, to the south-east of Falaise). The Seine was an intermediate defensive position. Hitler needed at least six weeks to prepare further defenses along the Somme, Marne, Saône, the Albert Canal and the Meuse. These defenses would stretch from the Channel to the Vosges. (DR)

Below: an 88mm Raketenwerfer 43, captured by American forces. By August 25 the Germans had lost more than 601 pieces of artillery in Normandy. (DR)

PRACTICAL INFORMATION

This list presents sites of historical interest in Calvados and neighboring regions. We are restricted to listing the most representative sites and those in the vicinity of the actual battlefields. Caen would be an excellent point of departure for any tour of the region.

CALVADOS

Five miles to the north of Caen, at Ouistreham, there is a **museum commemorating the landing of 4 Commando**. Uniforms, weapons and equipment are on display as well as documents relating to the landing of Anglo-French commandos at Sword Beach. The site is dedicated to the 177 commandos belonging to Kieffer's unit. There's also a monument alongside the D514, as it enters the south of the town, and another on the sea front.

Musée du débarquement des commandos n° 4
Place Alfred-Thomas
14150 Ouistreham
Tel.: 02 31 96 63 10

Further along the coast, 15 miles to the east, you arrive at Benerville-sur-Mer. Close by is **Mont Canisy**, transformed by the Germans into one of the most important batteries along the Atlantic Wall. There are numerous casemates, bunkers, observation posts and gun positions to visit as well as 20 miles of tunnels.

Site de la batterie du Belvédère au Mont Canisy
« Les Amis du Mont Canisy » - Mairie
14910 Benerville-sur-Mer
Tel.: 02 31 87 92 64 - Fax: 02 31 87 32 15

Opening hours: from April to October, Saturday and Sunday 14.30 to 17.30. There are free guided tours of the fortifications and installations- which last 2 hours. These are given by volunteers of the Friends of Mont Canisy. There is car parking. Bring a flashlight!

Turning back towards Bayeux, the **memorial museum to General de Gaulle** recalls the great man's visits to the city. It focuses on the visit of June 14, 1944 and that of June 16, 1946. There are numerous photos and documents on display and films are also shown.

Musée-mémorial du général de Gaulle
10, rue Bourbesneur
14400 Bayeux
Tel.: 02 31 92 45 55 - Fax: 02 31 51 28 29

Opening hours: March 15 to November 15, 09.30 – 12.30 and 14.00 - 18.30.

The **largest British cemetery** of World War II is to the south of Bayeux. It contains the graves of 4,648 Allied and German soldiers, of which 3,935 are British. Heading west along Route Nationale 13, the visitor will reach the vast **La Cambe cemetery**. Here 21,500 German soldiers lie buried beneath five huge black crosses. There's a memorial chapel at the entrance. Another German cemetery lies close by at Saint-Germain-du-Pert.

Five miles from there, on the coast, is the **Rangers Museum** at Grandcamp Maisy. It commemorates this elite American unit and its attack on Pointe-du-Hoc on D-Day.

Musée des Rangers
30, quai Crampon
14450 Grandcamp-Maisy
Tel.: 02 31 92 33 51 - Fax: 02 31 22 64 34
e-mail: Grandcamp-Maisy @wanadoo.fr

Heading along the D514 you reach Vierville-sur-Mer and the **museum for the Omaha landings**. It's an impressive collection of equipment, uniforms, artillery, weapons and even aircraft engines.

Musée D-Day d'Omaha
Route de Grandcamp
14710 Vierville-sur-Mer
Tel./fax: 02 31 21 71 80

Open between March 30 and November 10.

Some three miles further down the D514 is Coleville-sur-Mer with its **American Cemetery**. It covers 20 hectares and there are more than 9,000 white crosses. Most of the soldiers buried here were killed during the landing. There's a **memorial chapel** to American youth.

Further inland, some twenty miles to the south west of Bayeux is a **memorial museum** dedicated to the fighting in bocage country.

Musée de la Percée du Bocage
14350 Saint-Martin-des-Besaces
Tel.: 02 31 67 52 78

The association Les **Amis du Suffolk Regiment** organize guided visits in the area of Colleville-Montgomery, especially the Hillmann fortified site, a German command post with numerous underground casemates. This place was taken by men of Suffolk Regiment on June 7, 1944.

IN THE LA MANCHE REGION

Passing into the La Manche region on the RN 13 you soon reach the Carentan canal and then Sainte-Marie-du-Mont with its **Utah Beach museum**. It is the only museum dedicated to the landings there in the entire region and the exhibits are first class. Allied assault equipment and German defensive equipment are presented and videos are shown in three languages. There's a panoramic view over Utah Beach itself and Pointe-du-Hoc.

Musée du Débarquement d'Utah-Beach
50480 Sainte-Marie-du-Mont
Tel.: 02 33 71 53 35 - 02 33 71 58 00

Opening hours: from March 15 to November 15, 10.00 to 12.30 and 14.00 to 17.30.

Another fascinating site is 10 miles to the northwest at Crisbecq. It's the **German battery of Azeville and Saint-Marcouf**. There were four casemates here, armed with 105 mm artillery and eight blockhouses with a garrison of 170 artillerymen. There is also a flak position, underground bunkers and stores.

Batterie d'Azeville et de Crisbecq
« Les Cruttes »
50310 Azeville
Tel.: 06 63 11 60 20 - 02 33 40 63 05
Fax: 02 33 40 63 06

Access to the underground sites is only possible with a guide. Visits last 45 minutes.